Andrew Brodie Basics

LET'S DO PUNCTUATION

FOR AGES 10-11

- Structured punctuation practice
- Regular progress tests
- Matched to the National Curriculum

with over **100** reward stickers

Andrew Brodie
An imprint of Bloomsbury Publishing Plc

50 Bedford Square
London
WC1B 3DP
UK

1385 Broadway
New York
NY 10018
USA

www.bloomsbury.com

ANDREW BRODIE is a trademark of Bloomsbury Publishing Plc

First published in Great Britain 2017

Copyright © Andrew Brodie, 2017
Cover and inside illustrations of Andrew Brodie and Rufus the raccoon © Nikalas Catlow, 2017
All other inside illustrations copyright © Cathy Hughes, 2017

Andrew Brodie ... igns and Patents Act, 1988,
... k.

A catalogue record for this book is available from the British Library.

ISBN
PB: 978-1-4729-4081-0
ePDF: 978-1-4729-4080-3

2 4 6 8 10 9 7 5 3 1

Designed and typeset by Marcus Duck Design
Printed and bound in China by Leo Paper Products

This book is produced using paper that is made from wood grown in managed,
sustainable forests. It is natural, renewable and recyclable. The logging and manufacturing
processes conform to the environmental regulations of the country of origin.

To find out more about our authors and books visit www.bloomsbury.com.
Here you will find extracts, author interviews, details of forthcoming events and the
option to sign up for our newsletters.

BLOOMSBURY

T0347140

Notes for parents

What's in this book

This is the sixth in the series of *Andrew Brodie Basics Let's Do Punctuation* books. Each book features a clearly structured approach to developing and improving children's knowledge and use of punctuation in their reading and writing.

The National Curriculum states that children in Year 6 should learn appropriate terminology in relation to grammar and punctuation:

- statement
- question
- exclamation
- command
- full stop
- exclamation mark
- question mark
- capital letter
- comma
- brackets
- dash
- hyphen
- apostrophe
- speech marks
- inverted commas
- colon
- semi-colon
- bullet points

Note that some schools are instructing their pupils not to use the term 'speech marks' but only to use 'inverted commas'.

They will be reminded to punctuate their sentences with a capital letter at the start and a full stop, question mark or exclamation mark at the end. They will be using commas where appropriate to clarify meaning or to avoid ambiguity, as well as to indicate parenthesis – they will also use brackets or dashes for this purpose. Semi-colons, colons or dashes will be used to mark boundaries between independent clauses and colons will also be used to introduce a list, including a list of bullet points. The children will be using a capital letter for names of people, places, the days of the week, and the personal pronoun 'I'. They will be learning to use apostrophes to indicate where letters have been omitted or to indicate ownership, including

the possessive apostrophe with regular and irregular plurals. They will be punctuating direct speech by using inverted commas (speech marks) correctly. They will learn how hyphens can be used to avoid ambiguity (For example, dog-training instructor versus dog training instructor, or recover versus re-cover).

How you can help

Make sure your child is ready for their punctuation practice and help them to enjoy the activities in this book. If necessary, read the activity through out loud, discussing it so that your child really understands what the writing means. On every page there is a dotted circle where you can add a sticker to reward your child for working really hard.

The answer section

The answer section at the end of this book can be a useful teaching tool: ask your child to compare their responses to the ones shown. Their answers will not be identical but should include similar information. If your child has made mistakes, they can learn from these and do better next time. Remember that sometimes progress will seem very slow but at other times it can be surprisingly rapid.

Most importantly, enjoy the experience of working with your child. Together you can share the excitement of learning.

Look out for...

Rufus the Raccoon, who may tell your child what to focus on when working on the page.

Brodie's Brain Boosters, which feature quick extra activities designed to make your child think, using the skills and knowledge they already have. Can your child talk about their experiences using appropriate and interesting vocabulary? Can they then write well-punctuated sentences that give the information clearly?

Contents

Capital letters and full stops

Every sentence starts with a capital letter.

Most sentences end with a full stop.

Write the following sentences correctly.

yesterday i was given a new guitar for my birthday

_____

today i am going to practise playing my guitar

_____

tomorrow i am going to practise some more

_____

i am going to practise every day until i am really good at it

_____

i think practising is a very good practice

_____

some people need to practise the verb practise and the noun practice

_____

_____

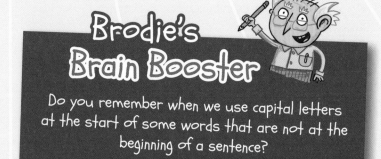

Brodie's Brain Booster

Do you remember when we use capital letters at the start of some words that are not at the beginning of a sentence?

Every name, day, month and title starts with a capital letter.

Write the following sentences correctly.

the train from inverness to london takes over nine hours

_____

the journey by car would take a little longer

_____

the flight from inverness direct to london takes one hour and twenty minutes

_____

_____

the flight from london to new york takes approximately eight hours

_____

_____

i would like to go to new york in may and to inverness in june

_____

charles dickens wrote a book called a tale of two cities

_____

my neighbour went to vancouver on saturday and she is going to sydney on wednesday

_____

_____

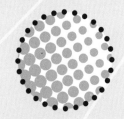

Brodie's Brain Booster

Can you find out which two cities Charles Dickens wrote about?

Questions

Every sentence starts with a capital letter.

Most sentences end with a full stop but some end with a question mark or an exclamation mark.

Write the following sentences correctly. Some of them are questions and some are not.

in what country is vancouver

_____

sydney is not the capital city of australia

_____

can you name six european countries

_____

what is the distance from london to inverness

_____

the flight distance from london to new york is 5585 kilometres

_____

what famous story about christmas did charles dickens write

_____

is it quicker to travel from london to new york by plane than to travel to inverness by train

_____

_____

Brodie's
Brain Booster

What is the capital city of Australia?

6

Creating questions

Don't forget capital letters, full stops and question marks.

An exclamation is a word or phrase that shows strong feelings, such as fear, surprise, excitement or anger.

Help! Wow! Brilliant! Watch out!

You probably noticed the exclamation marks.

Write some more exclamations. Don't forget the exclamation marks.

_____   _____

_____   _____

_____   _____

Sometimes, a whole sentence can end with an exclamation mark!

Rewrite the following sentences using correct punctuation, including an exclamation mark.

what a fantastic singer

_____

how brilliantly the dancers performed

_____

what terrible weather

_____

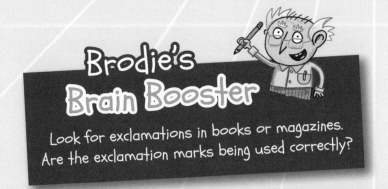

Brodie's Brain Booster

Look for exclamations in books or magazines. Are the exclamation marks being used correctly?

Hyphens

I hope you recover soon.

Shall we buy a new sofa or should we re-cover this one?

Hyphens are often found in compound words.

Notice the difference in meaning between the words recover and re-cover. The hyphen helps to clarify the meaning.

Now look at the next two examples. Write an explanation for each newspaper headline.

Dog-training instructor seeks new pupils.

_____

_____

_____

Dog training instructor to fetch ball.

_____

_____

_____

Brodie's Brain Booster

Find as many examples of hyphens as possible.

Using question marks

Can you work out where the question marks go?

Some of the sentences below should end with question marks. Put a tick by each sentence that must end with a question mark.

Tick four.

What a long journey it is from London to Inverness ☐

How far is it from London to New York ☐

Would you prefer to travel to Inverness by train or by plane ☐

How boring it is to travel on the motorway ☐

When is the next train to Inverness ☐

Who would like to travel to Australia ☐

What a lovely view from the train as we travel through the Highlands ☐

The journey across the Atlantic can be completed on a cruise liner ☐

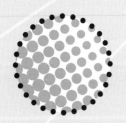

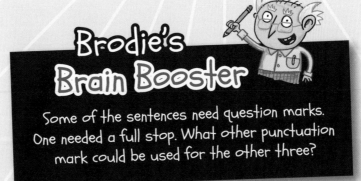

Brodie's Brain Booster

Some of the sentences need question marks. One needed a full stop. What other punctuation mark could be used for the other three?

9

The sentences below have been written incorrectly. Write them out correctly.

when are we going to glasgow

_____

i think we are going in june

_____

how are we going to get there

_____

we could travel by car, train or plane

_____

which method of transport are we going to use

_____

we will probably go by car

_____

One of the sentences below should end with a question mark. Put a tick by the sentence that must end with a question mark.

Tick one.

Ask at least one question every day ☐

Can I ask you how to make a cup of tea ☐

What a great cup of tea ☐

How tasty this biscuit is ☐

Apostrophes

Apostrophes can be used to shorten words where letters are missed out. Look:

we have ➡️ we've

This is an apostrophe.

The letters h and a in the word have have been omitted from we have to make the contracted form we've.

Write the contracted form of the underlined words in the boxes. It could help to read the words out loud.

"I <u>have not</u> finished my homework yet," said Phoebe.

⬇️
_____

"You <u>should have</u> started your homework as soon as you got home," said Dad.

⬇️
_____

"I know I <u>could have</u> done it then," said Phoebe, " but I <u>did not</u> think of it."

⬇️   ⬇️
_____   _____

"But <u>it is</u> obvious, Phoebe," said Dad.

⬇️
_____

"Well, it <u>was not</u> obvious to me at the time."

⬇️
_____

"I know," said Dad. "<u>I would have</u> done just the same thing when I was your age!"

⬇️
_____

Play script

Can you continue the script?

Read this short script. It contains lots of apostrophes.

Eli   Where're my tennis balls?

George   I don't know. Where d'you leave them?

Eli   I must've put 'em down somewhere.

George   Why don't you start in the kitchen?

Did you notice that we write the name of the speaker before we write what they say? Write a few more lines of the script. Will Eli find his tennis balls? You can decide.

_____

_____

_____

_____

_____

_____

_____

Brodie's Brain Booster

Try performing the full script with a friend.

Apostrophes for omissions

Letters have been omitted from some words in the sentences below. Write the underlined parts in full, in the boxes.

Eli <u>should've</u> kept his tennis balls in a safe place so he <u>wouldn't</u> lose them.

_____   _____

George <u>could've</u> helped him to look for the tennis balls.

_____

Eli tried the kitchen first but he <u>didn't</u> find the tennis balls there.

_____

George <u>hasn't</u> got much of an idea where to look because it <u>wasn't</u> him who lost the tennis balls.

_____   _____

Eli <u>won't</u> find them unless he looks properly.

_____

"I think <u>they're</u> in the garden," said George helpfully.

_____

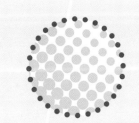

Brodie's Brain Booster

Be careful when omitting letters from **should have, would have, could have** and **must have.** They are contracted to **should've, would've, could've** and **must've** not should of, would of, could of or must of.

Possessive apostrophes

We also use apostrophes to show that someone owns something.

Look at this example:

My teacher's car has broken down.

The car belongs to the teacher. It is her possession. We call the apostrophe a possessive apostrophe.

Each line of the conversation below needs a possessive apostrophe. Some sentences also need apostrophes to show that letters have been omitted. Rewrite the conversation correctly.

have you seen amars new bike asked jasdeep

_____

i dont think its new said sophie it was his brothers

_____

its quite like dans said jasdeep

_____

whats dans like asked sophie

_____

its quite like amars said jasdeep grinning

_____

Brodie's Brain Booster

Look in the book you are reading. Can you find any possessive apostrophes?

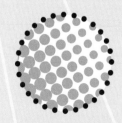

We can use possessive apostrophes when there is more than one owner.

Look at this example:

The women's clothes are on the ground floor of the shop.

We can tell that the clothes are for more than one woman. The clothes are for the women**, which is a plural word. The apostrophe is placed after the word** women**.**

Each sentence below needs two possessive apostrophes. Rewrite each sentence correctly.

we watched the mens rugby match first then we watched the womens

_____

the childrens clothes are on the same floor as the mens

_____

Now look at these plural words: adults   ladies   singers

With these words, the apostrophe goes after the whole word. Look at this example:

The singers' voices were in perfect harmony.

We can tell that the voices belong to more than one singer. The apostrophe is placed after the word singers**.**

Each sentence below needs two possessive apostrophes. Rewrite each sentence correctly.

we went through the adults clothes departments until we reached the girls clothes

_____

_____

the dancers costumes were even more colourful than the singers costumes

_____

Can you spot which sentences are correct?

Which sentence uses an apostrophe correctly?

Tick one.

The dance was performed by four people and all the dancers' costumes were different. ☐

The dance was performed by four people and all the dancer's costumes were different. ☐

The dance was performed by four people and all the dancers costume's were different. ☐

The dance was performed by four people and all the dancers costumes' were different. ☐

Write a sentence about the shorts belonging to the girls.

_____

_____

Write a sentence about the t-shirts belonging to the boys.

_____

_____

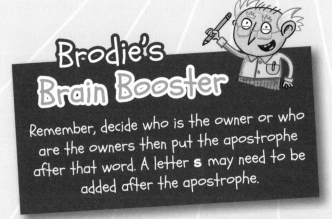

Brodie's Brain Booster

Remember, decide who is the owner or who are the owners then put the apostrophe after that word. A letter **s** may need to be added after the apostrophe.

Which sentence uses an apostrophe correctly when
we are writing about more than one teacher?

Tick one.

The teacher's cars are parked at the front of the school. ☐

The teachers car's are parked at the front of the school. ☐

The teacher's cars' are parked at the front of the school. ☐

The teachers' cars are parked at the front of the school. ☐

**Each sentence below needs two possessive apostrophes.
Rewrite each sentence correctly.**

The boys bike is the same type as his big brothers.

_____

Teds ball went into the pre-school childrens playground.

_____

The babies prams were lined up outside the schools front door.

_____

We borrowed Kates hamster cage because our hamsters cage is too
small. (one hamster)

_____

The ladies tennis tournament takes place before the mens.

_____

Inverted commas

"Your work is brilliant!" said the teacher enthusiastically.

"Thank you," I replied.

We use inverted commas to punctuate direct speech.

Rules for punctuating direct speech:

Inverted commas are written before and after the words spoken.	There is always a comma, a question mark, an exclamation mark or a full stop before the closing speech marks.	A new line is started when a different person speaks.

Rewrite the following conversation with the correct punctuation.

what work should i do next i asked write out a conversation suggested the teacher

_____

_____

Brodie's Brain Booster

Look in in a reading book. Can you find any written conversations?

Direct speech 1

We use inverted commas to punctuate direct speech.

Rules for punctuating direct speech:

Inverted commas are written before and after the words spoken.

There is always a comma, a question mark, an exclamation mark or a full stop before the closing speech marks.

A new line is started when a different person speaks.

Rewrite the following passage with the correct punctuation.

do you know the capital city of france asked seb of course i do replied jasmin what is it then continued seb paris said jasmin so what is the capital city of germany asked seb the capital city of germany is berlin said jasmin confidently

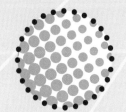

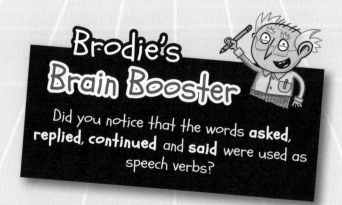

Brodie's Brain Booster

Did you notice that the words **asked**, **replied**, **continued** and **said** were used as speech verbs?

Direct speech 2

Can you think of other verbs we could use when we punctuate direct speech?

_____   _____

_____   _____

_____   _____

**Here is a short conversation without speech verbs.
Write an appropriate verb in each gap.**

"Where are you going?" _____ Mum inquisitively.

"To the park," _____ Eliza.

"Who are you going with?" _____ Mum.

"I think Sophie is coming," _____ Eliza.

"Anybody else?" _____ Mum.

"Zara is coming later but she is having her hair cut first,"

_____ Eliza.

"You need a haircut soon," _____ Mum.

"Do I have to?" _____ Eliza worriedly.

"Not if you don't want to," _____ Mum reassuringly.

Brodie's Brain Booster

Name the three adverbs used with the speech verbs.

20

Direct speech 3

Can you work out who is speaking?

Rewrite the following passage using the correct punctuation for direct speech. Notice that sometimes it doesn't say who is speaking and you need to work out who it is. Be careful, because some of the words are not spoken.

i can win this race said josh confidently i dont think you can said daisy i usually do insisted josh but you are not going to this time why not because i am going to win said daisy smiling cheerfully we will see about that said josh climbing on his bike ready asked daisy jumping on hers go shouted josh

_____

_____

_____

_____

_____

_____

_____

_____

_____

Brodie's Brain Booster

You could continue the story to show who won the race.

We sometimes write the speaker's name between two sentences.

Look at this example:

"I am going shopping this afternoon," said Jack.
"Do you want to come?"

In the example, Jack said both sentences.

Rewrite the following, splitting them into two sentences.

what time are you going asked harriet i might be able to come with you

_____

_____

the bus is late said tom crossly it is never on time

_____

_____

what time should the bus be here asked lauren it is nearly two o'clock now

_____

_____

the bus should have been here at one forty-five said james so it is over ten minutes late

_____

_____

never mind said molly i can see it coming up the hill now so we will soon be nice and warm

_____

_____

Brodie's Brain Booster

Have you used any form of public transport recently? Write a conversation that you could have with someone about your journey.

Quotation marks

We sometimes need to quote someone.

Inverted commas are sometimes called speech marks and they are sometimes called quotation marks, because we are quoting what someone said. We usually use single inverted commas when we are writing a short quote from what someone has said or written.

Look at this example:

Your work is so brilliant!

The teacher described the girl's work as 'so brilliant'.

Rewrite the sentences below. Try to spot the quotes and use single quotation marks around each of them.

the teacher said we should line up nicely but nobody did

_____

the headteacher said my picture was the best i have seen this term but i dont know if he meant it

_____

_____

scrooge said bah humbug about christmas because he did not want to celebrate the season

_____

_____

the sign on the gate said no entry so we did not feel very welcome

_____

**Rewrite the following passage
using the correct punctuation for direct speech.**

i beat josh in a bike race announced daisy excitedly you did not really win said josh frowning i certainly did insisted daisy but you started before i did i started as soon as you said go said daisy crossly but i wasnt ready said josh you shouldnt have said go then my foot slipped on the pedal said josh that is just your bad luck said daisy i definitely won the race

We can use commas to show exactly what we mean.

Look at the sentences below.

"I think we should change, Lily" said Maddie.

"I think we should change Lily," said Maddie.

In the first sentence the comma indicates that we should pause slightly. We can tell that Maddie is suggesting to Lily that they should change, perhaps to get ready for going out.

In the second sentence, there is no comma. Maddie is suggesting to someone else that they should change Lily in some way!

Here is another example of a pair of sentences meaning different things:

"Shall we eat Fiona?" asked Oliver.

"Shall we eat, Fiona?" asked Oliver.

What is wrong with the first of these two sentences?

_____

_____

What did Oliver mean really, as shown in the second sentence?

_____

_____

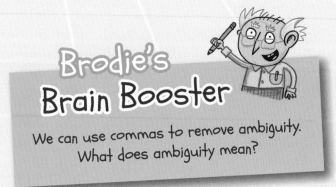

Brodie's Brain Booster

We can use commas to remove ambiguity. What does ambiguity mean?

Commas are often used after introductory phrases.

Look at these examples:

Without a doubt, the afternoon performance was better than the later one.

After we've eaten the first course, we'll have a short break.

I totally agree, the granary bread tastes better than the plain white loaf.

In each sentence, the comma encourages you to pause briefly as you read.

Rewrite the sentences below, punctuating them correctly and using commas in appropriate places. Each sentence only needs one comma.

after the summer holidays i'm moving on to secondary school

_____

the decision has been made you know which one you are going to

_____

after a lot of discussion weve settled on the one thats closest

_____

now that it is settled can we tell everyone

_____

no whatever happens don't let the cat out of the bag

_____

ive got to ask why is the cat in a bag in the first place

_____

Brodie's Brain Booster

Commas are also used to separate items in a list.

Commas in lists

Commas can be used to separate items in a list.

Look at this example:

The PE teacher bought new tennis balls, tennis rackets, tennis nets and kit bags.

In the list, there were four items:

tennis balls tennis rackets tennis nets kit bags

Did you notice that there were only two commas? The commas and the word and are used to separate the items.

Look at another example:

To make the cake I needed flour, baking powder, salt, butter, sugar, eggs and milk.

There were seven items in the list so there were five commas and the word and.

Rewrite the following sentences, punctuating them correctly.

the soup recipe listed carrots ginger turmeric pepper cream and vegetable stock

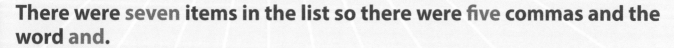

we had to remember our passports tickets and insurance documents when we went to france

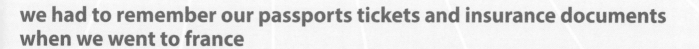

the shop sold a wide range of magazines most of the national newspapers and lots of different confectionery

Look at this example:

Our first lesson, straight after assembly, was maths.

The phrase straight after assembly **is not the main meaning of the sentence. It is giving extra information to make the sentence more interesting. The sentence could have just been:** Our first lesson was maths. **To separate the extra information, it is written between commas.**

Rewrite the following sentences with correct punctuation. It may help to read them out loud.

the journey to scotland broken only by a stop at the services took us over five hours

_____

_____

we were exhausted which was only to be expected so we went straight to bed

_____

_____

the next morning before we even had breakfast we went for a walk by the lake

_____

_____

we really enjoyed breakfast which was absolutely delicious and we were pleased to have the chance to relax until lunchtime

_____

_____

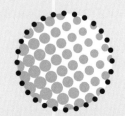

Colons to introduce lists

A colon consists of two dots and is often used to introduce extra information

 ⬅ **This is a colon.**

Look back through the book and you will find the colon used on most pages. It shows that something important is following. It is often used to introduce a list.

Look at this example:

We decided to take: a beach ball, a windbreak, a bucket and a spade.

Now look at this example:

We decided to take: the very large beach ball that we bought last year; a colourful windbreak with a mallet to knock the posts into the sand; a plastic bucket and a spade.

In both examples a colon introduces the list. In the second example, the items in the list are separated by semi-colons. This is because the items are so long and the semi-colons make the boundaries between them clearer.

You **can decide whether to use commas or semi-colons to make** your **sentence as clear as possible.**

Write a sentence about what you would like to buy on a shopping trip. Use a colon to introduce your list. Separate your items using commas or semi-colons as appropriate.

_____

_____

_____

_____

Colons are used to introduce bullet points.

Look at this example:

We decided to take:
- a beach ball
- a windbreak
- a bucket
- a spade

Did you notice that there was no punctuation apart from the colon and the bullets?

Now look at these examples:

We decided to take:
- a beach ball,
- a windbreak,
- a bucket,
- a spade.

We decided to take:
- a beach ball;
- a windbreak;
- a bucket;
- a spade.

Which one is right? They all are! You can choose how to set out the bulleted list but you must be consistent.

Write a bulleted list, introduced by a colon, about the presents you would like for your birthday.

_____

_____

_____

_____

_____

Brodie's Brain Booster

Look in a book, magazine or newspaper. Can you find a bulleted list? How is it punctuated?

Put a tick next to the sentence that shows Jamie is talking to Isla.

Tick one.

"Shall we go and check Isla?" said Jamie. ☐

"Shall we go and check, Isla?" said Jamie. ☐

Which sentence has been punctuated correctly?

Tick one.

As soon as the sun rose we leapt, out of bed, and headed to the beach. ☐

As soon as the sun rose, we leapt out of bed, and headed to the beach. ☐

As soon as the sun rose, we leapt out of bed and headed to the beach. ☐

As soon as the sun rose we leapt, out of bed and headed to the beach. ☐

Change the sentence below to a bulleted list.

There was a good selection on the breakfast menu: poached egg on toast; scrambled eggs on toast; porridge with syrup; bacon, sausages and eggs; corn flakes and beans on toast.

_____

_____

_____

_____

_____

_____

_____

Brackets

I have already mentioned bracketing commas.

Brackets can be used to enclose extra information in a sentence. Sometimes we choose to use commas and sometimes we choose to use brackets. **You have the choice.**

Look at these examples:

I had my last water pistol (a green one) for over two years.

I had my last water pistol, which was a green one, for over two years.

Both sentences give us the same information that the writer had owned her/his last water pistol for over two years and both have the extra information about the fact that it was a green one.

The sentences could also be written like this:

I had my last water pistol, a green one, for over two years.

I had my last water pistol (which was a green one) for over two years.

Write a sentence about a water pistol that can spray water up to five metres. Add extra information to say that it has a pirate sticker on the side of it. Choose whether you want to use brackets or commas.

_____

_____

_____

Brodie's Brain Booster

Look in your reading book. Can you find any brackets?

Dashes in pairs

Dashes can sometimes be used instead of brackets.

Dashes can also be used to enclose extra information in a sentence. Sometimes we choose to use commas, sometimes we choose to use brackets and sometimes we choose to use dashes. You have the choice.

Look at this example:

It was raining – pouring down, actually – so we found shelter in an old barn.

Did you notice that there is a comma after the word down, so it would not be good to use bracketing commas in this sentence. There would be too many commas. The dashes are a good choice.

Rewrite the sentences below, using dashes in appropriate places.

The sun was shining the first time for days so we went out and played in the garden.

_____

_____

The grass in our garden was very long too long actually so we went to the park to play instead.

_____

_____

Write a sentence of your own using a pair of dashes to give extra information.

_____

_____

Brodie's Brain Booster

Look in your reading book. Can you find any dashes used in a similar way to brackets or bracketing commas?

33

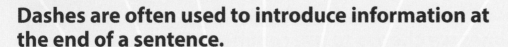

Dashes are sometimes used on their own.

Dashes are often used to introduce information at the end of a sentence.

Look at this sentence, which does not include a dash:

The largest animal in the world is the blue whale at up to thirty metres long.

Now look at this example:

The largest animal in the world is the blue whale – at up to thirty metres long.

Here, the dash has been used to emphasise what is coming next in the sentence.

Rewrite the sentences below. Use a dash in an appropriate place in each one. You may find you can miss out some words.

The highest mountain in the world is Mount Everest, which is 8848 metres high.

_____

_____

Yesterday we went to see a new film at the cinema brilliant!

_____

_____

It would be a good idea to take an umbrella it may rain later.

_____

_____

The water in the kettle has just boiled would you like a cup of tea?

_____

_____

Semi-colons

Semi-colons can sometimes be used in a similar way to single dashes.

Look at these examples:

My sister likes playing with Lego – my brother prefers watching television.

My sister likes playing with Lego; my brother prefers watching television.

Both sentences are punctuated appropriately. Perhaps the dash in the first sentence emphasises the contrast between the two activities. What do you think? Which do you prefer?

Rewrite the sentences below, punctuating them correctly. Each could have a dash or semi-colon to separate two clauses.

the television was on nobody was watching it

_____

there was plenty of food on the bird table not a single bird visited it

_____

the cat sat patiently under the bird table eventually she gave up

_____

the sandwiches were very nice the cakes were even better

_____

we watched a programme about the arctic later we watched a soap opera

_____

we walked all the way to the centre of town we got the bus back three hours later

_____

_____

Dashes to replace words

Dashes are sometimes used to replace words.

Dashes can be used in place of some words.

Look at this sentence:

I searched everywhere for the puppy but I couldn't find her anywhere.

Now look at this sentence:

I searched everywhere for the puppy – couldn't find her anywhere.

The dash emphasises that the searcher could not find the puppy.

Here is another example:

I asked my teacher what the homework would be and she said it would be spellings.

I asked my teacher what the homework would be – spellings.

Rewrite the sentences below. Use a dash in appropriate places to shorten each pair into one sentence.

My friend told me about her favourite hobby. She likes dancing.

_____

We went out on a boat and saw some exciting sea life. We saw dolphins and porpoises.

_____

_____

The weather changed quite suddenly. It became very wet and windy.

_____

Brodie's Brain Booster

Look in your reading book. Can you find any dashes used to miss out words?

Commas, brackets and dashes

You have lots of choices with punctuation.

Although there are rules for punctuation you also have some choices to make. **You** can decide when to use commas, when to use brackets and when to use dashes.

Rewrite the sentences below, using commas, brackets or dashes where appropriate.

The sea looked very inviting blue as cornflowers the tops of the waves glistening in the sunshine.

_____

_____

The water was very cold absolutely freezing so we didn't stay in for long.

_____

_____

We wrapped ourselves in our towels shivering with the cold then took shelter behind the windbreak.

_____

_____

After we had dried ourselves thoroughly we ran carefree on to the beach to play cricket.

_____

_____

We were so disappointed just an hour later when we had to pack our things and leave.

_____

_____

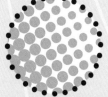

Rewrite the sentences below, using commas, brackets or dashes where appropriate.

The homework didn't take long about fifteen minutes but I was really pleased with what I did.

_____

_____

The tiger was enormous about three metres long but the enclosure at the zoo was quite large.

_____

_____

After the storm a frightening experience we all felt amazingly relieved.

_____

_____

Rewrite the sentences below. Use a dash in an appropriate place to shorten them into one sentence.

The snow was falling for about three hours so that the ground was completely covered. It was a beautiful sight.

_____

_____

Rewrite the sentence below. Use a dash or a semi-colon in an appropriate place.

We walked along the lane by the light of a full moon. Zoe was not frightened because it was so bright.

_____

_____

Practice pages

The name of every person, place, pet, day, month and title starts with a capital letter.

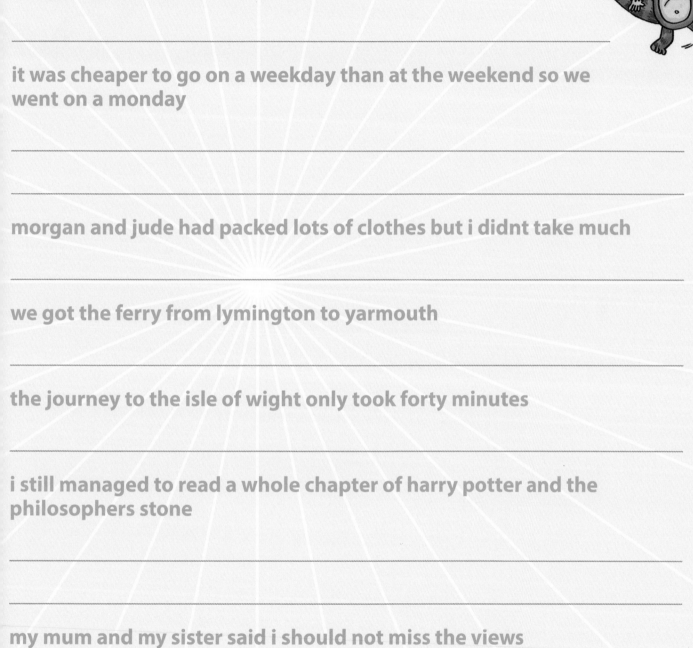

Write the following sentences correctly.

we made our first visit to the island in march

_____

it was cheaper to go on a weekday than at the weekend so we went on a monday

_____

_____

morgan and jude had packed lots of clothes but i didnt take much

_____

we got the ferry from lymington to yarmouth

_____

the journey to the isle of wight only took forty minutes

_____

i still managed to read a whole chapter of harry potter and the philosophers stone

_____

_____

my mum and my sister said i should not miss the views

_____

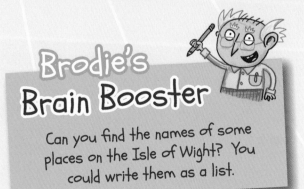

Brodie's Brain Booster

Can you find the names of some places on the Isle of Wight? You could write them as a list.

Practice pages

Every question sentence ends with a question mark

Every sentence starts with a capital letter.

Most sentences end with a full stop but some end with a question mark or an exclamation mark.

Write the following sentences correctly. Some of them are questions.

how many islands are there in the british isles

_____

there are over six thousand islands in the british isles

_____

the biggest of the islands is called great britain

_____

most of the islands are very small

_____

how many of the islands are inhabited

_____

two hundred and sixty seven of the islands are permanently inhabited

_____

_____

Brodie's Brain Booster

Find out which islands are closest to where you live.

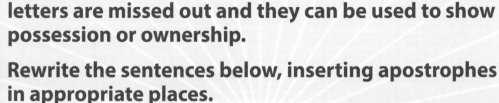

Apostrophes can be used to shorten words where letters are missed out and they can be used to show possession or ownership.

Rewrite the sentences below, inserting apostrophes in appropriate places.

i asked to use my friends pen but he was borrowing gemmas

_____

the blue whales diet consists almost totally of krill which are small crustaceans

_____

we couldve caught the isle of wight ferry in portsmouth or southampton instead of lymington

_____

_____

i looked in the tigers eyes and thought he didnt look very happy

_____

mum said that she wouldnt be happy if she lived in an enclosure like that poor tigers

_____

_____

there were three lions in the lions enclosure and they didnt look too happy either

_____

_____

Practice pages

Do you remember how to use inverted commas?

Rules for punctuating direct speech:

Inverted commas are written before and after the words spoken.	There is always a comma, a question mark, an exclamation mark or a full stop before the closing speech marks.	A new line is started when a different person speaks.

Rewrite the following passage with the correct punctuation.

what time are we getting the ferry i asked what does it matter asked jude im only asking i snapped back the ferrys at one oclock said mum thanks mum i said are we going to have lunch first asked jude what does it matter i asked grinning but she just ignored me it would probably be a good idea to have lunch first said mum unless we are going to get seasick exclaimed jude lets not think about that

Practice pages

Colons can be used to introduce information.

Rewrite the sentences below, using colons and commas in appropriate places.

my big sister jude packed lots of things to take to the isle of wight clothes board games magazines and loads of comic books

_____

_____

the music website features a large variety of genres pop hip-hop dance classical electronic and rock

_____

_____

Rewrite the sentences below, using colons and semi-colons in appropriate places.

we were required to practise several skills our ability to keep the ball in the air serving into the correct part of the court and using the backhand stroke

_____

_____

lots of volunteers are needed for the race every saturday morning people to scan the barcodes people to mark out the course and others to check the runners times

_____

_____

_____

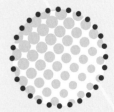

Practice pages

Colons can be used to introduce bulleted lists.

Rewrite the sentences below, changing them to bulleted lists. Don't forget that you will need a colon to introduce the bullet points, then you can choose whether to follow each item with a comma or a semi-colon or with nothing at all.

My teacher has a lot to do: preparing lessons, keeping us in order, marking work and drinking tea!

_____

_____

_____

_____

I have lots of ambitions: learning how to ski; getting better at tennis; writing my own book; acting in a film and buying my own car.

_____

_____

_____

_____

Brodie's Brain Booster

Write down your own bulleted list of ambitions.

44

Write the following conversation out correctly.

what would you like for supper asked mum i would like beans on toast fish fingers and chips cheesy pizza followed by ice cream with chocolate sauce please replied ali youre not getting all that said mum so which one will you choose could i have the pizza please asked ali certainly thats no problem said mum but please could i have the ice cream and chocolate sauce afterwards i suppose so

_____

_____

_____

_____

_____

_____

_____

_____

_____

Complete the bulleted list below correctly.

Ali asked her mum for: _____

_____

_____

_____

ANSWERS

Use the answers to check your child's progress but also to give prompts and ideas if they are needed. Note that sometimes your child's answer may not match the answer given here but could be just as good!

p4

Yesterday I was given a new guitar for my birthday.

Today I am going to practise playing my guitar.

Tomorrow I am going to practise some more.

Iam going to practise every day until I am really good at it.

I think practising is a very good practice.

Some people need to practise the verb practise and the noun practice.

Brain Booster:

Your child could list names, places, days, months, titles.

p5

The train from Inverness to London takes over nine hours.

The journey by car would take a little longer.

The flight from Inverness direct to London takes one hour and twenty minutes.

The flight from London to New York takes approximately eight hours.

I would like to go to New York in May and to Inverness in June.

Charles Dickens wrote a book called A Tale of Two Cities.

My neighbour went to Vancouver on Saturday and she is going to Sydney on Wednesday.

Brain Booster:

London and Paris.

p6

In what country is Vancouver?

Sydney is not the capital city of Australia.

Can you name six European countries?

What is the distance from London to Inverness?

The flight distance from London to New York is 5585 kilometres.

What famous story about Christmas did Charles Dickens write?

Is it quicker to travel from London to New York by plane than to travel to Inverness by train?

Brain Booster:

Canberra.

p7

Check your child's exclamations.

What a fantastic singer!

How brilliantly the dancers performed!

What terrible weather!

Brain Booster:

Help your child to find exclamation marks being used correctly.

p8

Dog-training instructor seeks new pupils.

This headline implies that a person who trains dogs is trying to find more dogs to train.

Dog training instructor to fetch ball.

This headline suggests that a dog is training its instructor to fetch a ball.

Brain Booster:

Help your child to find hyphens in use.

p9

How far is it from London to New York ✓

Would you prefer to travel to Inverness by train or by plane ✓

When is the next train to Inverness ✓

Who would like to travel to Australia ✓

Brain Booster:

An exclamation mark.

Progress Test 1

When are we going to Glasgow?

I think we are going in June.

How are we going to get there?

We could travel by car, train or plane.

Which method of transport are we going to use?

We will probably go by car.

Can I ask you how to make a cup of tea ✓

p11

haven't

should've

could've didn't

it's

wasn't

would've

p12

Check that your child has written an appropriate continuation of the script.

p13

should have would not

could have

did not

has not was not

will not

they are

p14

"Have you seen Amar's new bike?" asked Jasdeep.

"I don't think it's new," said Sophie. "It was his brother's."

"It's quite like Dan's," said Jasdeep.

"What's Dan's like?" asked Sophie.

"It's quite like Amar's!" said Jasdeep, grinning.

Brain Booster:

Help your child to spot possessive apostrophes.

p15

We watched the men's rugby match first then we watched the women's.

The children's clothes are on the same floor as the men's.

We went through the adults' clothes departments until we reached the girls' clothes.

The dancers' costumes were even more colourful than the singers' costumes

p16

The dance was performed by four people and all the dancers' costumes were different. ✓

Check your child's sentences.

Progress Test 2

The teachers' cars are parked at the front of the school. ✓

The boy's bike is the same type as his big brother's.

Ted's ball went into the pre-school children's playground.

The babies' prams were lined up outside the school's front door.

We borrowed Kate's hamster cage because our hamster's cage is too small.

The ladies' tennis tournament takes place before the men's.

p18

"What work should I do next?" I asked.

"Write out a conversation," suggested the teacher.

Brain Booster:

Help your child to find inverted commas.

p19

"Do you know the capital city of France?" asked Seb.

"Of course I do!" replied Jasmin.

"What is it then?" continued Seb.

"Paris," said Jasmin.

"So what is the capital city of Germany?" asked Seb.

"The capital city of Germany is Berlin," said Jasmin confidently.

Check that your child has used appropriate verbs.

inquisitively, worriedly, reassuringly

"I can win this race," said Josh confidently.

"I don't think you can," said Daisy.

"I usually do," insisted Josh.

"But you are not going to this time."

"Why not?"

"Because I am going to win," said Daisy, smiling cheerfully.

"We will see about that," said Josh, climbing on his bike.

"Ready?" asked Daisy, jumping on hers.

"Go!" shouted Josh.

Brain Booster:

Check your child's continuation of the story.

"What time are you going?" asked Harriet. "I might be able to come with you."

"The bus is late," said Tom crossly. "It is never on time."

"What time should the bus be here?" asked Lauren. "It is nearly two o'clock now."

"The bus should have been here at one forty-five," said James. "So it is over ten minutes late."

"Never mind," said Molly. "I can see it coming up the hill now so we will soon be nice and warm."

The teacher said we should 'line up nicely' but nobody did.

The headteacher said my picture was 'the best I have seen this term' but I don't know if he meant it.

Scrooge said 'bah, humbug!' about Christmas because he did not want to celebrate the season.

The sign on the gate said 'no entry' so we did not feel very welcome.

Progress Test 3

"I beat Josh in a bike race!" announced Daisy excitedly.

"You did not really win," said Josh frowning.

"I certainly did!" insisted Daisy.

"But you started before I did."

"I started as soon as you said 'go'," said Daisy crossly.

"But I wasn't ready," said Josh.

"You shouldn't have said 'go' then."

"My foot slipped on the pedal," said Josh.

"That is just your bad luck," said Daisy. "I definitely won the race."

The first sentence implies that Fiona is going to be eaten!

Oliver was asking Fiona if she was ready to eat.

Brain Booster:

Ambiguity means something is open to more than one interpretation. Ambiguity is inexactness.

After the summer holidays, I'm moving on to secondary school.

The decision has been made, you know which one are you going to.

After a lot of discussion, we've settled on the one that's closest.

Now that it is settled, can we tell everyone?

No, whatever happens, don't let the cat out of the bag.

I've got to ask, why is the cat in a bag in the first place?

The soup recipe listed carrots, ginger, turmeric, pepper, cream and vegetable stock.

We had to remember our passports, tickets and insurance documents when we went to France.

The shop sold a wide range of magazines, most of the national newspapers and lots of different confectionery.

The journey to Scotland, broken only by a stop at the services, took us over five hours.

We were exhausted, which was only to be expected, so we went straight to bed.

The next morning, before we even had breakfast, we went for a walk by the lake.

We really enjoyed breakfast, which was absolutely delicious, and we were pleased to have the chance to relax until lunchtime.

Check your child's sentence.

Check your child's bulleted list.

Brain Booster:

Help your child to find a bulleted list and to observe how it is punctuated.

Progress Test 4

"Shall we go and check, Isla?" said Jamie.   ✓

As soon as the sun rose, we leapt out of bed and headed to the beach.   ✓

There was a good selection on the breakfast menu:
• poached egg on toast;
• scrambled eggs on toast;
• porridge with syrup;
• bacon, sausages and eggs;
• corn flakes;
• beans on toast.

OR

There was a good selection on the breakfast menu:
• poached egg on toast
• scrambled eggs on toast
• porridge with syrup
• bacon, sausages and eggs
• corn flakes
• beans on toast

OR

There was a good selection on the breakfast menu:
• poached egg on toast,
• scrambled eggs on toast,
• porridge with syrup,
• bacon, sausages and eggs,
• corn flakes,
• beans on toast.

Check your child's sentence.

Brain Booster:

Help your child to search for brackets.

The sun was shining – the first time for days – so we went out and played in the garden.

The grass in our garden was very long – too long actually – so we went to the park to play instead.

Check your child's sentence.

Brain Booster:

Help your child to search for pairs of dashes.

The highest mountain in the world is Mount Everest – 8848 metres high.

Yesterday we went to see a new film at the cinema – brilliant!

It would be a good idea to take an umbrella – it may rain later.

The water in the kettle has just boiled – would you like a cup of tea?

The television was on – nobody was watching it.

There was plenty of food on the bird table – not a single bird visited it.

The cat sat patiently under the bird table – eventually she gave up.

The sandwiches were very nice; the cakes were even better.

We watched a programme about the arctic; later we watched a soap opera.

We walked all the way to the centre of town; we got the bus back three hours later.

p36

My friend told me about her favourite hobby – dancing.

We went out on a boat and saw some exciting sea life – dolphins and porpoises.

The weather changed quite suddenly – it became very wet and windy.

Brain Booster:

Help your child to find dashes that have been used to shorten sentences – quite a challenge!

 p37

Your child can choose to use commas, brackets or dashes. Here are the suggested answers:

The sea looked very inviting – blue as cornflowers – the tops of the waves glistening in the sunshine.

The water was very cold – absolutely freezing – so we didn't stay in for long.

We wrapped ourselves in our towels, shivering with the cold, then took shelter behind the windbreak.

After we had dried ourselves thoroughly we ran – carefree – on to the beach to play cricket.

We were so disappointed, just an hour later, when we had to pack our things and leave..

Progress Test 5

Here are some possible answers:

The homework didn't take long (about fifteen minutes) but I was really pleased with what I did.

The tiger was enormous – about three metres long – but the enclosure at the zoo was quite large.

After the storm – a frightening experience – we all felt amazingly relieved.

The snow was falling for about three hours so that the ground was completely covered - a beautiful sight.

We walked along the lane by the light of a full moon; Zoe was not frightened because it was so bright.

 p39

We made our first visit to the island in March.

It was cheaper to go on a weekday than at the weekend so we went on a Monday.

Morgan and Jude had packed lots of clothes but I didn't take much.

We got the ferry from Lymington to Yarmouth.

The journey to the Isle of Wight only took forty minutes.

I still managed to read a whole chapter of Harry Potter and the Philosopher's Stone.

My mum and my sister said I should not miss the views.

Brain Booster:

Help your child to look at a map or to research the Isle of Wight on the internet.

 p40

How many islands are there in the British Isles?

There are over six thousand islands in the British Isles.

The biggest of the islands is called Great Britain.

Most of the islands are very small.

How many of the islands are inhabited?

Two hundred and sixty-seven of the islands are permanently inhabited.

Brain Booster:

Help your child to find the information.

 p41

I asked to use my friend's pen but he was borrowing Gemma's.

The blue whale's diet consists almost totally of krill, which are small crustaceans.

We could've caught the Isle of Wight ferry in Portsmouth or Southampton instead of Lymington.

I looked in the tiger's eyes and thought he didn't look very happy.

Mum said that she wouldn't be happy if she lived in an enclosure like that poor tiger's.

There were three lions in the lions' enclosure and they didn't look too happy either.

 p42

"What time are we getting the ferry?" I asked.

"What does it matter?" asked Jude.

"I'm only asking!" I snapped back.

"The ferry's at one o'clock," said Mum.

"Thanks, Mum," I said.

"Are we going to have lunch first?" asked Jude.

"What does it matter?" I asked, grinning, but she just ignored me.

"It would probably be a good idea to have lunch first," said Mum.

"Unless we are going to get seasick!" exclaimed Jude.

"Let's not think about that."

 p43

My big sister, Jude, packed lots of things to take to the Isle of Wight: clothes, board games, magazines and comic books.

The music website features a large variety of genres: pop, hip-hop, dance, classical, electronic and rock.

We were required to practise several skills: our ability to keep the ball in the air; serving into the correct part of the court and using the backhand stroke.

Lots of volunteers are needed for the race every Saturday morning: people to scan the barcodes; people to mark out the course and others to check the runners' times.

 p44

My teacher has a lot to do:
• preparing lessons,
• keeping us in order,
• marking work,
• drinking tea!

OR

My teacher has a lot to do:
• preparing lessons;
• keeping us in order;
• marking work;
• drinking tea!

OR

My teacher has a lot to do:
• preparing lessons
• keeping us in order
• marking work
• drinking tea

I have lots of ambitions:
• learning how to ski;
• getting better at tennis;
• writing my own book;
• acting in a film;
• buying my own car.

OR

I have lots of ambitions:
• learning how to ski,
• getting better at tennis,
• writing my own book,
• acting in a film,
• buying my own car.

OR

I have lots of ambitions:
• learning how to ski
• getting better at tennis
• writing my own book
• acting in a film
• buying my own car.

Brain Booster:

Check your child's bulleted list.

Progress Test 6

"What would you like for supper?" asked Mum.

"I would like beans on toast, fish fingers and chips, cheesy pizza, followed by ice cream with chocolate sauce please," replied Ali.

"You're not getting all that!" said Mum, "So, which one will you choose?"

"Could I have the pizza please?" asked Ali.

"Certainly, that's no problem," said Mum.

"But please could I have the ice cream and chocolate sauce afterwards?"

"I suppose so."

Ali asked her mum for:
• beans on toast,
• fish fingers and chips,
• cheesy pizza,
• ice cream with chocolate sauce.

OR

Ali asked her mum for:
• beans on toast;
• fish fingers and chips;
• cheesy pizza;
• ice cream with chocolate sauce.

OR

Ali asked her mum for:
• beans on toast
• fish fingers and chips
• cheesy pizza
• ice cream with chocolate sauce